ABOUT PADSTOW

MICHAEL WILLIAMS

BOSSINEY BOOKS

Published in 1993 by Bossiney Books, St Teath, Bodmin, Cornwall

Typeset and printed by Penwell Ltd, Callington, Cornwall

© Michael Williams 1993

ISBN 0948158 85 9

ACKNOWLEDGEMENTS:

Front cover photography: ROY WESTLAKE
Front cover design: MAGGIE GINGER
Other photographs: RAY BISHOP.
Old photographs kindly lent by Mrs MARGARET ROWE

Author's Acknowledgements
I wish to thank the Strand Bookshop for commissioning this publication and Margaret Rowe and her daughter Pat Bate for all their help and encouragement. I am also indebted to Brenda Duxbury, my co-author of *The River Camel*. That now out-of-print Bossiney title has provided valuable background material. Also thanks to the Cornish Studies Library at Redruth, and Terry Knight in particular, Trevor England for reading the sea section, Angela Larcombe for her editing, the various photographers, especially Ray Bishop, Maggie Ginger for her cover design, Mrs Tarry's permission to quote Claude Berry's words and Sally Dodd for typing the manuscript. Last, but not least, I owe a special debt to the Rev Barry Kinsmen, the Rector of St Issey and St Petroc Minor, who has read the manuscript.

Books Consulted:
The River Camel, Brenda Duxbury & Michael Williams, Bossiney, 1987; **Saints of the South West**, James Mildren, Bossiney, 1989; **Portrait of Cornwall**, Claude Berry, Robert Hale, 1974; **Claude Berry's Padstow**, edited by Donald Rawe, Lodenek Press, 1976; **The Folklore of Cornwall**, Tony Deane & Tony Shaw, Batsford, 1975.

About the Author

MICHAEL WILLIAMS, a Cornishman, started full-time publishing in 1975. He and his wife Sonia live in a cottage on the shoulder of a green valley just outside St Teath in North Cornwall.

In addition to publishing and writing, Michael Williams is a keen cricketer and collector of cricket books and autographs. He was the first captain of the Cornish Crusaders Cricket Club and is today President of the Crusaders. He is also a member of Cornwall and Gloucestershire County Cricket Clubs – and a Vice-President of the Cornwall Rugby Football Union. A member of the International League for the Protection of Horses and the RSPCA, he has worked hard for reform in laws relating to animal welfare. In Cornwall he is a Patron of the Broomfield Horse Sanctuary at Penzance.

In 1984 he was elected to The Ghost Club, and remains convinced Cornwall is the most haunted area in all Britain. His contributions to the Bossiney List include Paranormal in the Westcountry *and* Supernatural Investigation.

Now in words and pictures he explores Padstow. The home of the 'Obby 'Oss Festival, the haunt of famous Westcountry seadogs in the past, Padstow is a treasure chest of Cornish history and folklore.

This, Bossiney's 216th title, has been commissioned by the Strand Bookshop of Padstow.

3

About Padstow

'SOME think of the farthest away places as Spitzbergen or Honolulu. But give me Padstow, though I can reach it any day from Waterloo without crossing the sea. For Padstow is in Cornwall and Cornwall is *another* country.'

That was Sir John Betjeman's London impression more than forty years ago.

Padstow is essentially Cornish – as Cornish as the pasty or Bishop Trelawny.

You could not mistake Padstow for a Devon or indeed any English town or port. It has that character and quality which set Cornwall and the Cornish a place and a people apart.

I vividly remember my first visit to Padstow: the narrow winding streets, the harbour, the smell of fish, the call of the gulls, and those glorious views across to the golden sandy beaches on the other side of the water. In the right light you get this brilliant combination of gold and blue.

Here is how an Edwardian visitor described her arrival at Padstow:

'After quitting the train, we find the approach to the town from the station a remarkable one. We walk along the stony track by the line, which is usually cumbered with trucks; between us and the river are sheds, heaped with boxes, barrels and baskets, either containing fish, or intended for fish, or just emptied of fish. The notion seizes us that we are not on British ground at all, but have reached some small Continental seaport and are humbly progressing towards the Custom House. The fact that ere long we do pass the Custom House adds to the impression. Then we emerge upon the North Quay. The scene at high tide is pretty enough; small vessels of different builds sway one against another; there is some desultory loading or unloading going on; idlers loiter about enjoying the aspect of other people's activity, and under the hill little low buildings of a more or less maritime character are clustered together. We turn a corner, find an unpretentious post office; light upon Ye Old Shippe Inn with a carved wooden sign, and an antiquated air, not at all in keeping with the fact that it is a temperance hotel. It rather suggests sack or Canary, or the Jamaica rum of a later time. There are some shops – we at first get the impression that they all sell picture post-cards; but, like other

Sir John Betjeman, the former Poet Laureate, who lived on the other side of the estuary: a man who had known this corner of North Cornwall since boyhood holidays.

first impressions this is erroneous. Narrow streets run upwards, interlaced by yet narrower ones: by and by we realize that this is the whole of Padstow, assuredly one of the quaintest, oddest little towns in all the kingdom.'

The railway, of course, changed the face of Cornwall in that it brought the holiday-makers, and sowed the seeds of expanding tourism. The most concrete reminder of that in Padstow is the Metropole Hotel, originally named the South Western Hotel, built in 1900 by the Corys, a well-known shipping family.

The Metropole boasts magnificent views over the great, sandy sweep of the Camel.

Today there is no railway line, no Padstow station; but tourism remains a vital plank in the local economy. Naturally the rail traveller from earli-

Looking down from Dennis Hill, the footpath, where once trains travelled along the track from Wadebridge to Padstow.

er this century would see big changes today. Development with a capital D, cars and more cars, more people, television aerials, yellow lines, all these have changed the character of the place – but only to a certain degree. Despite it all, Padstow retains a certain individuality, and the thousands of visitors who come here – many on return visits – are confirmation of its magnetism.

As a Cornishman born and bred, I enjoy Padstow best out of season, and if you want an out-of-season break in Cornwall you could not make a better choice. In fact the weather in spring and autumn is often the best in the calendar.

The name Padstow is a corruption. Over the years it has been known by a variety of titles. Once it was Petroc-stow – Petroc's Church – an even older name was Lanwethinoc – the monastery of Wethinoc. It has also been known as Lodenek – the fortified inlet – a title remembered down to Leland's time around 1535. And in the Middle Ages it was Aldestow – the old church.

If you stand on the 'Obby Oss' slip when a strong westerly is blowing, you would hardly know it: a perfect setting for the harbour tucked around the corner from the open sea and sheltered from prevailing westerlies by a steep hill behind.

This was the end of the line … Padstow Station.

7

Little wonder St Petroc chose this spot after his crossing from Wales some 1400 years ago. The stories and legends surrounding him are many. He came of a noble family in Wales, but did not wish to inherit his father's kingdom. Instead as a youth he went to Ireland to study under renowned Christian teachers. Inspired to spread the Gospel he sailed to Cornwall arriving in a boat not much bigger than a Welsh coracle. Perhaps he landed at Trebetherick and there met the reapers who taunted him to demonstrate his holiness. St Petroc is reputed to have struck the rock with his staff and immediately a fountain of the purest water flowed.

St Petroc

SABINE Baring-Gould considered him *'the man who left a deeper impress on the west . . . than any other saint.'* He founded a great community here at Padstow before moving on to Bodmin, the religious capital of Cornwall down to the end of the Middle Ages. James Mildren in his *Saints of the South West,* published by Bossiney in 1989, profiled Petroc in these words:

'Petroc was also an exceptional administrator and he died at Treravel, on the way from Nanceventon to Lanwethinoc in June 564. Many wonderful tales are told about this loveable man who, it is said, was even kind to dragons! He originated in Gwent, and belonged to the royal house there. The ivory casket, decorated with Arabic workmanship, which once contained his bones, was, happily, returned to Bodmin Church in October 1957. But his bell disappeared shortly before the reign of King Henry I, and was never recovered.'

Some of the old folk believed there were more saints in Cornwall than in heaven. So perhaps it's no surprise to find more than two hundred churches in ancient Kernow. Churches, like inns, tell us a good deal about the past. Provided we are receptive enough, every church has something to tell us about earlier religious and secular life in Cornwall, and the Church of St Petroc here at Padstow is no exception.

The exact site of St Petroc's monastery is debatable. Some say it is where the church stands now. Others believe it was higher up at Prideaux Place where St Samson, yet another Cornish saint, lived as a hermit. But the large shaft and base of a cross near the south east gate of

St Petroc, who made his Cornish base at both Padstow and Bodmin.

the churchyard, found when digging a grave, perhaps indicate the church and monastery were both here.

In the turbulent years before the Norman Conquest, the coasts of Britain suffered greatly from Viking raids and Cornwall was no exception. The monastery at Padstow was destroyed by the Vikings in 981; its valuables made it a ready target. The *Anglo Saxon Chronicle* records the disaster. '*In this year S Petroc's stowe was sacked and the same year very great damage was done everywhere by the coast in Devon and Cornwall.*' The monastery almost certainly ended in flames and the monks removed to Bodmin.

It is this event that Anya Seton, the historical novelist, chose as central to her novel *Avalon,* set in the last quarter of the tenth century: a period of conflict between Church and State, and the threat of Viking invaders. It is a vivid, fast-moving piece of fiction with enough historical research to give us a glimpse of North Cornwall nearly a thousand years ago.

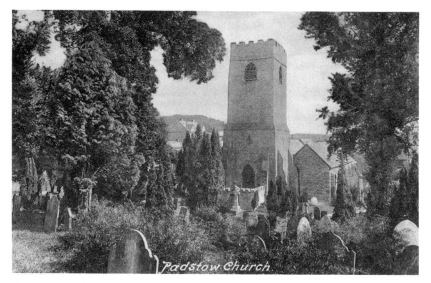

A postcard depicting Padstow Church, sent by a visitor in 1927 to a friend in Salisbury.

The Church

THE present parish church, high above the town, is set in a gentle green hollow framed by trees, surrounded by grey headstones. It is mainly fifteenth century and there is plenty to see here. In the church you will find eight-holed wooden stocks. A form of punishment worth reintroducing for young offenders perhaps?

Inside there is a finely carved fifteenth century font bearing the figures of the twelve Apostles – made of dark catacleuse stone from the cliffs hard by Harlyn Bay. There was an ancient theory that anyone baptised in it would never go to the gallows. However the theory failed to work for a man called Elliott. He was christened here but was hanged about 1800 for robbing the mail.

Some old buildings, especially churches, generate a spirit of the past – not a vague spirit either but one seemingly peopled by personalities from former days – and Padstow Church is such a place.

On the steps of the sanctuary is the engraved brass of Laurence Merther who was vicar here in the 1400s. Against the south aisle wall is an impos-

Padstow Church: much of the building is fifteenth century, the tower has a thirteenth-century base and the arcades are a century later. Below: The neatly kept churchyard.

ing monument to the Prideaux family: the kneeling figures of Sir Nicholas Prideaux (dated 1627), his wife and four sons; father in armour and sons in long capes and ruffs. The monument also commemorates William Morice, who married Sir Nicholas's grand-daughter; knighted when Charles II landed at Dover, he was made Secretary of State for his services in the Restoration.

There is some fine stained glass. You can see King Edmund with arrows, Michael with burning sword, and Nicholas with a vessel. There are also three women saints with scenes from their careers: Catherine discussing – probably disagreeing – with doctors, Winifred sewing, and Cecilia with her husband and an angel. Not forgetting St Petroc himself in the modern east window carrying his Abbot's crozier.

Prideaux Place

UNTIL 1538 the Prior of Bodmin was Lord of the Manor of Padstow, the last being Prior Vivian, whose tomb lies in the sanctuary of Bodmin Parish Church. It was during the sixteenth century at the time of the Reformation when Henry VIII confiscated the great estates of the monasteries, that the lands of St Petroc's original monastery came into the possession of the Prideaux family, and Sir Nicholas instructed builders to start work on the mansion that became Prideaux Place. Soon it was a place of importance in the county with the Prideaux family playing a major role in the affairs of Cornwall. It was seemingly little troubled during the Civil War. The family were staunch Parliamentarians.

Probably the most famous of the family was Humphry Prideaux. Educated at Westminster School, he was elected to Christ Church, Oxford, and became a highly respected scholar. In 1702 he was appointed Dean of Norwich, and despite serious illness – he underwent major surgery long before the invention of anaesthetics and the surgeon botched the job – he made valuable contributions to theological research. He died in 1724 and his tomb appropriately is inside Norwich Cathedral.

Cornwall has her share of great houses. Such grand residences not only add to the quality of our Cornish landscape but the people who lived in such properties – often on the scale of hotels – had a deep influence on the affairs of Cornwall: men who represented Cornwall in Parliament or served as High Sheriffs and women, whose duties and influence went far

When Arthur Mee toured Cornwall in the 1930s he wrote 'Prideaux Place is one of those lovely sights that come upon us suddenly in our countryside'.

beyond their households.

With embattled and creepered walls, projecting bays and mullioned windows, Prideaux Place remains today Padstow's most imposing residence. Trees and parkland are rare sights in North Cornwall but here at Padstow a half circle of trees protects the manor, the church and the former borough of Padstow from the prevailing westerlies. You can obtain a good view from the road to Tregirls, and if you're lucky you will actually see deer in the park. This, of course, is one of the few manor houses in Cornwall still lived in by the family who built it. There is an interesting legend to the effect that when the deer leave Prideaux Place, the Prideaux-Brune family will leave it too.

For four centuries Prideaux Place has been the home of the Prideaux family who can be traced back to Prideaux Castle, Luxulyan at the time of the Norman Conquest in 1066. Present owners are Peter and Elisabeth Prideaux-Brune, direct descendants of Sir Nicholas Prideaux, the man who built the original Elizabethan mansion. Succeeding generations

13

have, of course, embellished and extended the property. Filled with quality porcelain, portraits and furniture, Prideaux Place is open to the public on many days during the season, but it remains essentially a family home with the majority of the rooms still in regular use.

Among the special features are some very fine carvings by Grinling Gibbons, a fireplace and staircase from the Grenville House at Stowe, just across the border in Devon, and some pictures by John Opie, Cornwall's most famous portrait painter. When only a boy, dressed in a plain jacket, Opie, the son of a carpenter at St Agnes, arrived at the house one morning and proceeded to paint the entire family, including the pet dogs. Later Opie returned home, dressed in a handsome coat, lace ruffles and silk stockings, gleefully producing twenty guineas and predicting that, in future, he would support himself. It was no idle boast, for though Opie's career was to have its troughs, his best work won golden opinions, Sir Joshua Reynolds once saying, 'This youth begins where most artists leave off . . .'

It was Queen Elizabeth I who granted Padstow borough status but the Prideaux family objected fearing a reduction in their power, and Padstow corporation subsequently disappeared. But not before one Ann Calwoodly caused a scene in the church. A new pew had been installed for the mayor and the lady reacted vehemently to the extent of bringing an axe to church to smash the pew to pieces. She was brought before the Court of Star Chamber, but we do not know her fate.

May Day

CERTAIN occasions set Cornwall apart. The 'Obby 'Oss festivities at Padstow every May Day is one of them. Like hurling at St Columb and the Floral Dance at Helston, it gives Cornwall that special indefinable something.

Tony Deane and Tony Shaw in *The Folklore of Cornwall,* published by Batsford in 1975, opened their May chapter with these words:

The Golden Lion, where the 'Old 'Oss is kept. This inn has a special ▶ *place in the history of Padstow. Padstow folk make their way to stand outside the inn just before midnight and as the last chime fades from the church bells, they begin to sing. It's May Day!*

The 'Obby 'Oss – a tradition that continues today.

'The night-singing at Padstow is an experience that can only be appreciated by those who have taken part in it. No-one could fail to be impressed by the haunting air sung in the pitch-dark by massed, unaccompanied voices and the sheer pleasure in the performance.'

Padstow recaptures an exciting spirit every May Day: crowds and ancient customs turn the narrow streets into a cauldron of activity. The old town breathes an atmosphere of sheer theatre: the music, the singing and the dancing, the excited crowds, the eating and the drinking all mingle with tradition, as do Padstonians and outsiders.

Messrs Deane and Shaw in the same May chapter had this to say:

'Documentary evidence of Padstow's 'Obby 'Oss reaches back only as far as the beginning of the nineteenth century, but there is a widespread impression that its history is much longer. One story suggests that the horse dances in memory of the women of Padstow who, when their menfolk were away at sea, donned red cloaks to convince a marauding French battlefleet that the British army was waiting on shore: certainly, one stanza from an earlier version of the song substantiates this theory . . .'

The Hobby Horse – or 'Obby 'Oss to the true Cornish – is a fearsome animal wearing a fierce mask, making him resemble a heathen God

16

rather than a living horse. Before the horse dances a local man, carrying a club, called 'the teaser'. One spectator observed: 'the whole thing is grotesque, but is one of the most genuine folk customs surviving . . .'

The 'Obby 'Oss is, in fact, a man encased in a cloth mask, grimly black, save for the various coloured stripes on his cap and mask. He wears a tall cap with a flowing plume and tail and savage-looking wooden snappers. The cap, plume, tail and decoration of the snappers are all made of genuine horsehair. Jaws of the snapper are studded on the inside to multiply the noise, and these are operated by a string held by the man inside the 'Oss.

The Cornish historian, Thurstan Peter, thought the ceremony and the Helston Furry Dance to be *'pagan festivals of revivals and fruitfulness, and one of those forms of magic, not by any means implying the notion of invariable cause and effect, but an attempt to express in ritual the emotions and desires – and so to this have been grafted on the one-hand folklore and on the other Christian ceremonies, the history being still further confused by mistaken efforts of well-meaning persons to remove elements*

'Oss and Teaser on the great day in 1949. The drummer on the left, wearing spectacles, is David Farquhar, former Rock-Padstow ferryman and later bookseller at the Strand.

17

A photograph from the Rowe family album. This group was pictured in the old market, and, below, a later picture from the album shows ladies collecting money for the Blue Ribbon 'Oss, probably in the late 1960s. Mrs Margaret Rowe is second from the left, standing holding a collecting box, alongside her daughter Sally.

18

regarded by them as coarse.'

Perhaps though it needs an outsider to set the scene vividly. Raymond Gardner, visiting the town for *The Guardian* in 1975 did just that with these words on the morning of the great day:

'And now Padstow sleeps fitfully in expectation of the summer rite to come. Walk quietly through the streets and you will hear, from behind the occasional lit window, the first strains of another song. it is the last practice. Then the children emerge in the long shadows of the sunrise. Down through the twisting alleys, out through the arches, and into the public courtyards they come, in their garlands of flowers. Some carry branches of May, each is dressed in white and sports the red or blue sashes of the 'oss they will follow. By 7am the two Children's 'Osses and the young Mayers are outside the Metropole Hotel and the well-heeled tourists are quickened from sleep by the persistent humming of the drums and the shrill call of the accordion.

'This is a preliminary. At 10am the crowd meets before the Institute. The Mayers have assembled – the men with their accordions, melodions, tambourines, and drums are poised for the song, the master of ceremonies struts about in top hat and tails, the Teazer appears with his clubs. Suddenly the Blue Ribbon 'Oss is upon us, whirling like a dervish, rearing against the crowd, his great hooped skirt lashing as he abandons himself to the dance and the Teazer's twitching hands. Stand back and let the beast have his moment. Stand firm and you may spend the remainder of your holiday gazing from the windows of the cottage hospital where they do a nice line in mending split skulls.

There are, in fact, two main 'Osses. The blue ribbon, who started life as the peace 'Oss after the 1914-18 war and the long established Old 'Oss, traditionally smaller, presumably to go through the narrow passage of its stable, Padstow's oldest inn the Golden Lion – a tight squeeze before refurbishment a few years ago.

Claude Berry

IT WAS my great-aunt Mabel Williams – the headmistress in A.L. Rowse's first book of autobiography – who introduced me to Claude Berry.

A real all-rounder, Claude Berry was a writer, broadcaster and journal-

Claude Berry, a distinguished son of Padstow: author, broadcaster and journalist. He was a reporter for the Cornish Guardian, *spent six notable years in Fleet Street, before his health broke down and he returned to his native land: first to Bodmin and later to Truro where he was for many years the editor of the* West Briton.

20

ist; above all he was a Padstow man. Writing in the Padstow and District Guide of 1957, he said:

'I have known Padstow, and the district for miles around, for more than half a century.

'Yet, whenever I return, the first glimpse of the town and harbour from highroad or railway never fails to fill me with gratitude that I was born and bred in a town so comely and interesting in itself; and so superbly part of its beautiful and romantic setting along the coast of North Cornwall: easily one of the grandest and most fascinating in the British Isles. But if I sometimes envy the newcomer because he comes quite fresh to a scene that I have known intimately for so long, and grow to love more passionately as the years go by, I am also intensely glad that my mind is stored with memories of this ancient little port "in the roar of the sea".'

His broadcasts – from what we called the wireless in those days – portrayed the reality of Cornish life. In a 1943 broadcast, for example, Claude Berry recalled the problems of the family surviving on his father's wage of £1 a week as a carpenter in pre-war days. He played for his school team in ordinary boots without studs because they could not afford to buy him a pair of real football boots. Then came crowning humiliation: selection for his first away match: a fare of two and sixpence. He eventually blurted out the truth to his sports master: they couldn't afford that kind of money. '. . . he put his hand on my shoulder and piloted me to the study door – "You're outside right on Saturday, and every Saturday." ' In Claude's words: 'He paid, and I played. I won a friendship that day which was broken only when, a soldier myself in France, I heard he'd been killed in the war.'

Stephen Fuller

ANOTHER distinguished son of Padstow was Stephen Fuller. His early death robbed the town of a great worker – and ambassador. In his short life Stephen Fuller gave himself without stint, serving Padstow and its people.

He loved music, especially Cornish carols and folk songs, and hymns of Sankey and Moody – and he was a loyal member of his church. He was the creator and driving force of the *Padstow Echo*. Professor Charles Thomas, writing in the memorial issue to its founder, said: *'With*

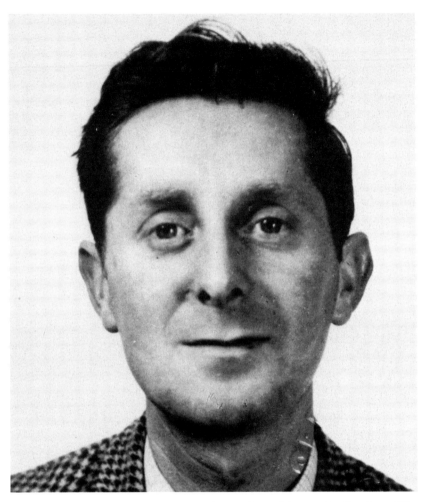

Stephen Fuller of Padstow who, throughout his tragically short life, gave himself unstintingly to Cornwall and Cornish causes.

Stephen's passing, Cornwall as well as Padstow is the poorer. The Echo is, in every sense, his memorial . . . Stephen never pretended to be other than Cornish, a Padstow man and a man of the people. This was his editorial standpoint, and it was the right one, at a period when so much that he counted worthwhile was being threatened.'

In the same edition of the *Echo*, Robert Dunstone, President of Mebyon

In 1972 the Cornish Bard Ernest Morton Nance pays tribute to Stephen Fuller. The seat here is dedicated to Stephen's memory.

Below: The Cornish historian Dr A.L. Rowse, at the same ceremony unveils the memorial tablet on the Claude Berry shelter on the North Quay. On the left are Gordon Dawe, the Mayor of Padstow, and Mrs Winifred Berry.

Kernow, reflected 'Stephen was one of those people who quite properly became a Bard of the Cornish Gorseth by sheer hard work and merit . . . Not for nothing did Stephen choose as his bardic name 'Son of Fisherman' . . . he was the son of a fisherman, and he lived in a fisherman's family, and in a fisherman's town.'

The Strand Bookshop

AS A publisher and author I have a special regard for the Strand
Bookshop here in Padstow. Not only does it embody all those qualities
of the old-fashioned bookshop, it was one of our very first customers
when we launched into publishing back in the 1970s - it has gone on giving us first-class support ever since - the commissioning of this title
being the latest example of that support.

In 1986 the bookshop acquired a kind of literary fame. You will find it
inside the pages of a romantic novel, entitled *Impulsive Challenge* writ-
ten by Margaret Mayo, and published by Mills and Boon.

Gisele, the central character in the novel, visits Padstow:

'. . . *Another hour was spent in a bookshop on the Strand. It was filled
from floor to ceiling in glorious disarray. As well as new books and
paperbacks there were secondhand and antiquarian books on almost
every subject under the sun. Books about Cornwall, maps, prints. It was
a fascinating shop and Gisele could have stayed there all day, except
that she was afraid Catherine might worry if she did not return soon.'*

As a member of The Ghost Club, and someone who has been investi-
gating the supernatural for more than a quarter of a century, I was especially interested to hear this account from Margaret Rowe in the autumn
of 1990. It concerned the Strand Bookshop and this is what she told me:

'It was late in August 1990 and only a few minutes from closing time.
We keep open until ten o'clock in the season, and this lady came in. She
was wearing a white top and black skirt - very modern type of dress -
and she went to the back of the shop to look at some books out of of
view. When ten o'clock came, the three of us thought it was time to
close. We'd had a long day, but when we went to tell the lady it was
closing time, she simply wasn't there. We even went upstairs to check
that she might have wandered off up there. But no sign of her anywhere.
All I can tell you is she came into the shop, but she didn't go out!'

Getting back to the bookshop side of things, in April 1993 I was asked
to write something about the Strand Bookshop for the *North Cornwall
Advertiser*. Here are three paragraphs from that article.

*'The Strand Bookshop has been an important part of the book scene in
North Cornwall for nearly 30 years: one of those treasured features - a
Cornish business run by Cornish people.*

The Strand Bookshop in 1987: Michael Williams with Margaret Rowe and her daughter Pat Bate.

'It was in 1964 that David Farquhar, a well-known Padstow character, started business at The Strand, and it was then taken on by his sister Margaret Rowe - and today the family tradition flourishes in that her two daughters and grand-daughter are involved in the business.

'Spring 1993 sees the beginning of an important new chapter for the shop; refurbished and recently re-opened it has gone back to the old beams - so the original character is retained. But with the wonderful bonus of more space for more books.'

Shortly after the reopening of the Strand Bookshop in April 1993: left to right: Michael Williams, Pat Bate and Dawn Jones.

Padstow around 1920: a drawing by Heather Griffiths.

The Harbour

THOUGH an island race, inland people are inclined to take the excellence of our harbours and ports for granted.

The fact is the growth of harbours help to fashion the character and style of the personalities and the places around them - and Padstow is such a case. The skill of our Cornish ship and boat builders and the audacity of our mariners are vital ingredients in the story - and stories of Cornwall.

Leo Walmsley was right. 'Seaports and harbours cannot be mass-produced.' Of course, they have a good deal in common in terms of pure

27

Paddle boat at Padstow watched by a solitary lady – this was before the building of the new pier.

activity, but, at heart, they are individual.

In the 1700s a map was inscribed with these words: *'Padstow: by its Situation at the Mouth of the River Camel in the Bristol Channel, lies very convenient for Commerce with Ireland. The Inhabitants of this Town, for the Love of Mirth and Good Cheer, give rise to the proverbial phrase of the Good Fellowship of Padstow.'*

Padstow, in those days, was one of the ports from which men and supplies had gone to the Irish wars - and from Padstow two ships sailed to the siege of Calais.

Padstow was, of course, the haunt of great Westcountry seadogs. Sir John Hawkins, for example, in 1565 found shelter here from the autumn gales on his return from the West Indies. Later Sir Martin Frobisher, returning from his quest for the North West Passage to China, was also relieved to find shelter here. Sir Walter Raleigh came too.

On the south quay stands Sir Walter's Court House. As Warden of the Stannaries of Cornwall, he held his court here, collecting legal dues. The Queen showered favours upon him, including responsibility for the rich Cornish mines.

Another old building, which stirs curiosity and speculation, is Abbey House on the North Quay, from which a subterranean passage was built; a theory links it with the ill-fated monastery. Abbey House is believed to have been the Guild House of the Padstow merchants. A large chunk of Padstow's history has been related to the sea: trading, fishing and ship-building. The Guild of St Petroc was created to finance joint stock fishing ventures.

Abbey House is reputed to house a gentle ghost. It is an interesting fact that many ghosts 'reside' by water, the sea or rivers. Peter Underwood in his excellent *Ghosts of Cornwall* first published by Bossiney in 1983, devotes a fascinating chapter to Padstow's 'other population'.

Times were - medieval times - when all Padstow, including the harbour, belonged to the Priory of Bodmin. Consequently harbour tithes were paid

Historic Abbey House photographed in November 1942. The ancient railings were scheduled to be scrapped for metal – part of the war effort – but on Government orders they were retained.

Ray Bishop captures the magic of Padstow Harbour on a fresh April morning.

Many of the old picture postcards had a beautiful visual quality. Here is a card of Padstow Harbour.

to the Abbot. In Chaucer's day Padstow was an important destination for pilgrims travelling from Wales and Ireland to Rome. The pilgrims would land here and then travel across Cornwall to Fowey or St Michael's Mount for re-embarkation for Europe - others would go direct to the Mediterranean by sea. Not surprisingly many Irish people lived in the town. Coasting vessels also traded up the Bristol Channel and across to Brittany.

Around the middle of the sixteenth century John Leland, the King's Librarian, researching his Survey of England, came to North Cornwall and noted that many Breton ships were here exchanging French goods for Padstow fish.

In the seventeenth and eighteenth centuries trade increased with the expansion of mining - copper, antimony and lead ores being included with other exports of grain, cured fish and slate. The port handled imports from Ireland of glass and linen, salted pork and callow linen and canvas came from Brittany and salt, wine and vinegar also from France: malt and hardware from the Severn ports. But it was in the nineteenth century that the main expansion took place. Timber was then brought from Scandinavia and from as far as Canada. These same ships, on their outward journeys, took to the New World these immigrants from the Old, victims of the agricultural and mining slumps of the nineteenth century.

In her heyday Padstow harbour must have been a wonderful sight - the quays packed and larger vessels moored in the Pool, the deep water anchorage beyond; brigs and brigantines, smacks and schooners, barquentines and square riggers. Padstow then boasted several shipbuilding yards.

But the passage of time inevitably brought changes - big changes to the harbour and the town.

The advent of iron and steam ships killed boatbuilding in Padstow, but the beginning of this century saw a revival in the fishing industry, not only among local boats. The East coast drifters made Padstow their centre for winter fishing of the 'Klondike', the name given to the rich fishing grounds off the North Cornish coast. With the coming of the railway fish could be sent direct to London. This, too, was the era of the ice factory on the quay.

Superstition and the sea have long been close relations. And Padstow fishermen were no exceptions. A *West Briton* report, published in December 1848, said: *'Within the last few weeks the fishing boats of Padstow have caught several thousands of herrings, but one boat being more unfortunate than the others, some persons persuaded the crew that the boat was bewitched. They then determined to break the charm by nailing a horseshoe to the bottom of the boat, which they did, and the next night caught 1,400 fish, which confirmed the belief that the boat had been bewitched!'*

The Doom Bar

ALL OF which leads us naturally to the Doom Bar, that great grim sandbank across the mouth of the estuary.

Mermaids feature strongly in the folklore of Cornwall, and legend has an explanation for the Doom bar which precludes Padstow's natural harbour from shipping of really great size. The harbour, once deep and open, had been a mermaid's playground. However, one foolish fisherman tried to shoot her and, in revenge, the mermaid cursed Padstow by placing this sandbar across the entrance.

The Doom Bar may give shelter from the Atlantic swell for the modern

32

Here is another postcard, this time of the Padstow lifeboat crossing the Doom Bar in a gale. Posted from Padstow and addressed to Mrs R. Williams of Heamoor, near Penzance, the message reads: 'Hope you are not feeling lonely. We are going for a drive this afternoon with a lady. Lovely here.'

dinghy sailor, but it has been literally doom for hundreds of vessels wrecked here. The coast of North Cornwall can be wicked: no other harbour of any size apart from Hartland, Newquay and St Ives, and none of these offer a haven in a northerly gale or at low tide. As a result, vessels caught out in rough weather have frequently tried to find refuge here – only to be driven on to Doom Bar.

Smuggling and Wrecking

NO publication on Padstow can be complete without some reference to smuggling.

First, though, one must scrape away much of the romantic glitter surrounding many of the stories. Times were when smuggling followed fish, tin and copper as the leading Cornish industries, but as for the smugglers themselves, the majority were men soaked in violence and corruption –

33

Herbert Hughes was a gifted photographer who visited Cornwall in the early 1900s. Here he photographs Harbour Cove in 1907, with the Padstow lifeboat and a Padstow registered steamer.

even murder.

It is fair to say the deep poverty – and it was deep – of the fishermen and miners was alleviated by goods and cash from the 'trade'. The smugglers were cunning in that they advised local people when their contingent travelled through the village, they should face the wall. Consequently if smugglers were arrested the villagers could, with hands on heart, say they had seen nothing.

'Them that ask no questions isn't told a lie, watch the wall, my darling, while the gentlemen go by.'

Even the great John Wesley tried to stir the Cornish conscience on the subject. 'A smuggler then,' he said, 'and in proportion, every seller or buyer of uncustomed goods is a thief of the first order, a highwayman, or a pickpocket of the worst sort.'

Conscience or no conscience, this stretch of Cornish coast was notorious, and St Minver and St Merryn, in that order, were rated the top 'plac-

34

ing' districts in North Cornwall. One wreck at Polzeath had a cargo of sugar and rum. Something like a hundred casks of rum crashed against the rocks, and the spirits mingled with salt water in the hollows. Apparently there was much drunkenness. So much so that a man, named William Ham from Carvath, St Austell, who was working at Wadebridge at the time, drank so much that a local doctor was called. He employed a stomach pump, but without success.

John Wesley & Methodism

THE Methodist buildings and the Methodist people in and around Padstow are reminders of John Wesley and his message. He hit Cornwall and the Cornish like a storm-force gale.

Here in North Cornwall you cannot escape John Wesley and you cannot begin to understand Cornwall without reference to him. Without Methodism vital pieces are missing. We are Celts: emotional and instinctive. Religion of a kind is bred into the bone. In Cornwall Wesley won converts by the hundred. 'Many of the lions are become lambs . . .' he wrote in his Journal. North Cornwall – like the rest of ancient Kernow – is punctuated with chapels, legacies and his fiery message. In the high noon of Methodism these buildings rang with 'Alleluyas'.

And after Wesley came a whole army of Nonconformist preachers. Congregations, like those of the Church of England, may have declined, but the flame of Methodism still burns in many Cornish hearts, and Mr Wesley himself would approve of today when the relationship between Methodists and Anglicans is warm and friendly.

Here is a glimpse into the old style of chapel: Edwin Chapman recalling an important occasion and later changes at the Padstow Wesleyan Chapel in the *Padstow Echo* of 1968:

'I remember attending the Memorial Service to the late Queen Victoria in the year 1901.

'It being such an impressive and sad occasion, one wonders why it seemed fitting for a child of my tender years, about 7 yr's old, would find such a Service suitable; I must have thought otherwise as sitting or standing I could not see choir or preacher – the address seemed endless, so I contented myself counting the lights in the beautiful STAR which was then overhead in the centre of the ceiling, the lighting system (gas)

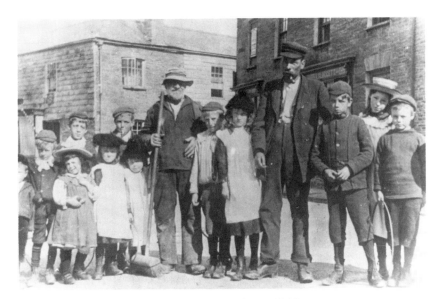

A group pictured in Market Square, about 1910.

was at that time very attractive; at various seat or pew corners are still to be seen the rounded base ends from which the twisted brass pedestals with their lovely rounded globes of lights were installed. In after years this system of lighting was replaced by groups of four mantle gas lighting, with additional wall lighting, then, sometime later in the 1920's electric lighting was installed with large bowl centre lights etc., one can reflect now as to the beautifully placed lighting originally installed to the more practical of the present day.'

The Cruel Cornish Sea

THERE is in Padstow a tombstone covered with lichen and it says quite simply on the '30th day of November' Samuel French was 'unfortunately drowned in discharge of his duty.'

121 years later, in 1992, a double blow struck the town. First, the population was stunned by the loss of two local fishermen, Arnold Murt and Bronco Harding on a night fishing trip. Then only days later another three Padstow fishermen, Paul Masters, his cousin David Masters, and

A piece of Padstow sea history: the steam lifeboat Helen Peele, *and, below: an old photograph of Trevose Lighthouse.*

Peter Hope all perished on another fishing expedition.

These two tragedies brought sharply into focus the traditional problems of balancing the demands of working at sea with those of sheer survival.

Anthea Hall, writing in the *Sunday Telegraph*, on December 6 1992, said: *The recession, the demands of the EEC regulations and a dreadful season threaten to drive fishermen to the edge of seamanship and to renewed risks.'*

Padstow is such a community that when there is a tragic loss of life the town is bereaved like one big clan.

Here at Padstow a brave and distinguished lifesaving tradition has developed over the years. The 1820s saw the first lifeboats.

First sited in Padstow, the lifeboat was later stationed at Hawker's Cove nearer ships in distress. No effort was too much in those days for they would even transport the lifeboats on carriages to launch at the beach closest to the vessel in danger. This meant a a shorter distance to

The former Duchess of Kent meets members of the crew of the Padstow Lifeboat in May 1952, when she launched a new boat.

Looking down to the harbour. It was on Padstow Harbour that I was interviewed by Colin Wilson in 1972 for the first colour television film made in the Westcountry.

row. The Lifeboat Station can still be seen at Hawker's Cove, although many will remember in more recent times, the *Joseph Hiram Chadwick* anchored in the Pool off Padstow, in order that she might always be afloat. The increased silting up of the Bar stopped her getting out easily at low water; so, at an estimated cost of £114,600 a new Lifeboat Station was built on the east side of Trevose Head in the open sea. Here the Duke of Kent in 1968 unveiled a commemorative plaque.

'From the cliff platform the Duke admired the impressive views of the North Cornwall coast,' wrote a Cornish Guardian *reporter. 'Because of the strict timetable he was advised not to go down to the station, and after looking at the hundred or so concrete steps he would have to descend and ascend, he added jocularly:*

'Perhaps it is just as well, after lunch!'

Here the new lifeboat can be launched swiftly at any state of tide in a bay protected from the prevailing wind and swell by the Merope Rocks. It is a dramatic sight to see the lifeboat travel down a 240 foot slipway to join the Atlantic.

Earlier on the same day in 1968 the Duke, deputising for his mother

39

Princess Marina who had gone into hospital, named at Padstow the new lifeboat *James and Catherine Macfarlane*. '. . . *it was a split-second affair'*, observed the same *Guardian* journalist, the lowest tide of the year *'gave the large lifeboat only a few inches of clearance under her keel as she rocked gently in the inner harbour.'*

In 1984 Padstow received a new lifeboat, the *James Burrough*. She is 47 feet in length and the third of the very up-to-date Tyne class boats, with steel hull, aluminium superstructure, and seven watertight compartments all of which make her inherently self-righting. With a speed of 18 knots, twice as fast as the *James and Catherine Macfarlane*, she has an effective range of 250 miles offshore. This speed is possible because the Tyne class lifeboats have a flat transom and are fitted with trim tabs enabling the boat to lift almost on to the plane rather than having to throttle back in heavy seas. The crew of seven have to be strapped in as she is a very lively potent boat. Complete with the latest communications technology, she has achieved seventeen rescues in fourteen months.

In April 1986 on a pitch black night she went to the help of a yacht *Seagoe* twelve miles offshore which was taking in water. A tow was secured. Her master stated that the crew would remain on board insisting that they were going to be all right. Within five minutes she sank, the lifeboat crew having to quickly cut the tow. Coxswain Trevor England, who holds two RNLI silver decorations for bravery, manoeuvred the boat to pick up within six minutes all four cadets, the master and the owner without hitting anyone in the water. Even in that short time the sailing master became too cold to grab the line and one of the lifeboat crew had to jump into the sea and grab him. Six lives were saved that night due to superb seamanship and teamwork, adding to the reputation of Padstow lifeboat, which, over the years, has effected some incredibly brave rescues.

Disaster though has struck twice. The first time was in 1867, when the second *Albert Edward* was called out to rescue the crew of a schooner which had been driven on to the Doom Bar. With gigantic waves running astern, she was swept along towards the schooner, when her drogue – the big canvas cone astern, employed to prevent 'somersaulting' – suddenly tore away. An enormous wave caught the boat aft and hurled her forward and over. All thirteen members of the lifeboat crew were thrown into the raging surf. Eight of them, exhausted yet alive, made the shore.

40

The topsail schooner Katie *built at Padstow, one of the last of the coastal sailing traders, photographed here at Par Harbour.*

But the bodies of the five others were later found on rocks and in the dark gullies of Hell Bay, perhaps a more appropriate name for Hayle Bay.

One, who perished that day, was a man of remarkable courage. He was Daniel Shea, Chief Officer of Coastguards, who on retiring as coxswain on his promotion to Chief Officer, had continued to serve as a volunteer. Richard Tyacke, the then vicar of Padstow, referred to 'the brave Mr Shea', who had served two Padstow lifeboats and had helped in 'the saving of 45 lives'. A giant of a man – he was over six feet tall – Daniel Shea won the RNLI silver medal and three other distinctions for gallantry in life-saving, including a medal especially struck by the Emperor of France for his heroic skill in rescuing the crew of a French ship wrecked near Padstow. He was only 42 when he died and was described by a journalist as 'almost a legendary figure not only in North Cornwall, but in the England of mid-Victorian times'.

The other Padstow disaster took place on the fateful night of 11 April

An Edwardian stroll on a breezy day, judging by the way the lady clutches her hat.

These lads find the stile a good place for viewing the scene.

1900. This time, eleven men were lost including eight lifeboat men, and one trawler and two lifeboats were wrecked. One of these was the new *James Stephens*, the first steam lifeboat which had been in service for just over a year. The trawler *Peace and Plenty* had dragged her anchor under Stepper during a vicious gale. She blew across the estuary in a maelstrom of surf grounding on Greenaway rocks where the Trebetherick rocket brigade managed to save all but three of her crew. Meanwhile the alarm had been raised on the Padstow shore and the old lifeboat, the *Arab*, was rowed through the surf to the other side of the estuary using a back channel round the bar. They searched in vain in the dark, and losing all but three oars, the boat too ended on Greenaway rocks, the crew scrambling to safety. Meanwhile, in answer to their flares, the *James Stephens* steamed out to Stepper and once clear of the Bar turned towards Polzeath. There she was hit by a gigantic sea on her quarter that knocked her broadside to the waves. She capsized with all but three of her crew drowned.

There was nearly a third disaster in 1944 when Bill Orchard won the silver medal for gallantry and the award for the bravest lifeboat man of the year. It was on November 23 that the *Princess Mary* was called out. She was the largest lifeboat in service, and as her coxswain and second coxswain were newly appointed, it was Bill who took the helm. It took them only three hours to reach Knap Head near the Devon and Cornwall

43

Tregudda Cliffs: the rocks around Padstow seem picturesque to the visitor but can threaten the lives of those who go to sea.

border where the Norwegian vessel, *Sjofna,* was on the rocks. She was carrying a cargo of china clay from Fowey to Larne in Ireland. The Clovelly lifeboat was already standing by but could not approach her as she was lying inside the breakers under the high cliffs. Large waves were breaking over her and the crew were huddled on the bridge. 'Somebody just had to do something', said Bill. 'The men on the top of the cliff had been trying to fire a line to the boat but without success.'

With the coming of dawn, Bill anchored the lifeboat to seaward, then veered warp gradually so as to drift stern first towards the wreck. Heavy seas broke on their bows injuring one of the lifeboat crew. Bill had to give full power as each wave struck the boat in order to take the strain off the warp, thus enabling the anchor to hold.

Two lines were fired over the wreck but the crew were unable to make them fast, so Bill re-anchored in a new position closer to the *Sjofna.* This brought the lifeboat into even shallower water. Two more lines were fired as the lifeboat struck bottom in the troughs. But this time the line was secured and a breeches buoy rigged, seven of the *Sjofna's* crew

An earlier view of Padstow when masts still dominated the scene.

being brought to safety across the surf before the line chafed through.

As the tide cropped so the Hartland Life-Saving Apparatus Company managed after sixteen hours of trying, to get a line aboard. In the process the Captain had his leg broken by one of the rockets but eventually the rest of the crew were hoisted to safety up the cliff.

Yes, a long and distinguished tradition at Padstow, and when such people sing the *Sailor's Hymn* every word comes from the bottom of the heart.

> *Eternal Father, strong to save,*
> *Whose arm doth bind the restless wave,*
> *Who bidd'st the mighty ocean deep*
> *Its own appointed limits keep:*
> *Oh hear us when we cry to thee*
> *For those in peril on the sea.*
>
> *O Trinity of love and power,*
> *Our brethren shield in danger's hour;*
> *From rock and tempest, fire and foe,*
> *Protect them wheresoe'er they go:*
> *And ever let there rise to thee*
> *Glad hymns of praise from land and sea.*

W. Whiting, 1825-78

But perhaps the last words should come from Arnold Murt, one of those local fishermen who died in 1992. Arnold, the Vicar said, called it 'God's wonderful country' – and, of course, he meant *Padstow.*

MORE BOSSINEY BOOKS ...

CURIOUS CORNWALL
by Michael Williams
Words and pictures prove Cornwall has more than her share of things curious.
'... what insights, words of wisdom about Cornwall and the Cornish experience ... not in any forced manner or through any artificial device of compression. I suppose it all arises from a life of interest in and experience of the Cornish scene.'   Dr James Whetter, **The Cornish Banner**

STRANGE STORIES OF CORNWALL
Six writers prove that fact is often stranger than fiction.
'Thought-provoking ... little-known odd occurrences, strange places and eccentric characters.'   Adrian Ruck, **Cornish & Devon Post**

THE CRUEL CORNISH SEA
by David Mudd
David Mudd selects more than 30 Cornish shipwrecks, spanning 400 years, in his fascinating account of seas and a coastline that each year claim their toll of human lives.
'This is an important book.'   Lord St Levan, **The Cornish Times**

DAPHNE du MAURIER COUNTRY
by Martyn Shallcross
A special look at Cornwall in which the internationally-famous novelist set important stories.
'A treasure chest for those who love Cornwall and the du Maurier novels.'
Valerie Mitchell,   **The Packet Group of Newspapers**

OLD PICTURE POSTCARDS OF CORNWALL
by Sara Paston-Williams

GHOSTS OF CORNWALL
by Peter Underwood
Peter Underwood, President of the Ghost Club, journeys across haunted Cornwall. Photographs of haunted sites and drawings of ghostly characters all combine to prove that Cornwall is indeed a mystic land.

PARANORMAL IN THE WESTCOUNTRY
by Michael Williams

MORE BOSSINEY BOOKS ...

MYSTERIES IN THE CORNISH LANDSCAPE
by Tamsin Thomas

DISCOVERING BODMIN MOOR
by E.V. Thompson

LEGENDS OF CORNWALL
by Sally Jones

SUPERNATURAL INVESTIGATION
by Michael Williams
Investigations into a whole range of Supernatural subjects: ghosts and ghostly music, dreams and time slips, superstition and theatre ghosts.

MYSTERIES OF THE SOUTH WEST
by Tamsin Thomas of BBC Radio Cornwall
'Complete with dozens of photographs and drawings, Tamsin Thomas presents a fascinating word-picture tour.'   **North Cornwall Advertiser**

NORTH CORNWALL REFLECTIONS
by Hilda Hambly

KING ARTHUR IN THE WEST
by Felicity Young and Michael Williams

BODMIN MOOR THROUGH THE YEARS
by E.V. Thompson

GHOSTLY ENCOUNTERS
by Peter Underwood

We shall be pleased to send you our catalogue giving full details of our growing list of titles for Devon, Cornwall, Dorset and Somerset as well as forthcoming publications. If you have difficulty in obtaining our titles, write direct to Bossiney Books, Land's End, St Teath, Bodmin, Cornwall.